823 HUX 20177

ALDOUS HUXLEY

LUTON SIXTH FORM COLLEGE

4 NOV 1999

1 4 SEP 2018

This book is due for return on or before the
last date shown above.

3123

¶ALDOUS LEONARD HUXLEY was born at Godalming, Surrey, on 26 July 1894. He died in Hollywood, California, on 22 November 1963.

ALDOUS HUXLEY

ALDOUS HUXLEY

by

JOCELYN BROOKE

PUBLISHED FOR
THE BRITISH COUNCIL
BY LONGMAN GROUP LTD

LONGMAN GROUP LTD
Longman House, Burnt Mill, Harlow, Essex

*Associated companies, branches and
representatives throughout the world*

First published 1954
Revised 1958, 1963
Reprinted with minor corrections 1968, 1972
© Jocelyn Brooke 1958, 1963, 1972

*Printed in Great Britain by
F. Mildner & Sons, London, EC1R 5EJ*

SBN 0 582 01055 1

ALDOUS HUXLEY

ANY comparison between Aldous Huxley and H. G. Wells
must seem, at first glance, impossibly arbitrary and
far-fetched: for surely no two writers—considered
merely as writers—could be more dissimilar. Yet such a
comparison is, I think, not only justified but, as a matter of
literary history, almost unavoidable.

For those who came to maturity during the first two decades of the present century, the most potent intellectual
influence was probably that of Wells; it was an influence
which might be resisted but could hardly be ignored by any
up-to-date young man of the period. Wells was not only
the first and greatest of the scientific popularizers; he was
also a prophet and a revolutionary, and his perky, dis-
respectful attitude to 'respectable' institutions, combined
with an immensely readable style, seemed to his younger
contemporaries to typify the intellectual climate of the time.

How different, it may well be objected, was the case of
Huxley: aloof, fastidious and, by contrast with Wells's
bouncing optimism, profoundly a pessimist; upper-class
both by birth and disposition, whereas Wells was plebeian
and proud of it; preoccupied largely with problems of
pure æsthetics and, latterly, with mysticism, for both of
which Wells would have felt little but an amused contempt.
Yet, viewed in a wider context, the similarities between the
two men can be seen to outweigh their differences: for
Huxley was also a popularizer, not only of æsthetic and
philosophic, but also (like Wells) of scientific, ideas; he
too—though in a somewhat different sense—was both a
revolutionary and a prophetic writer; and, most notably,
he was, like Wells before him, the 'typical' writer of his
generation, and a major influence upon the young intelli-
gentsia of his time.

His importance, in this last respect, can hardly be exaggerated, though there is a very natural tendency among the
youngest generation to underestimate it. For those who,
like the writer of the present essay, were growing up during

the 1920s, Aldous Huxley seemed unquestionably the most stimulating and exciting writer of the day: his style in itself was a novelty—highly-wrought yet extremely readable, deriving from unfamiliar models, and providing a refreshing contrast to that of such older writers as Galsworthy, Bennett, and Wells himself. Huxley was gay, sophisticated and (for those days) agreeably shocking; but more important, for his young readers, was the impact of an alert, penetrating and widely-ranging intelligence. By comparison, most other contemporary writers seemed stuffy, unenlightened and old fashioned.

The effect was intoxicating: like the great Knockespotch, that imaginary genius described in *Crome Yellow*, Huxley had 'delivered us from the dreary tyranny of the realistic novel'; like Knockespotch, again, he preferred to study the human mind, not 'bogged in a social plenum', but 'freely and sportively bombinating':

'Oh those Tales—those Tales! [exclaims the eloquent Mr Scogan] How shall I describe them? Fabulous characters shoot across his pages like gaily dressed performers on the trapeze. There are extraordinary adventures and still more extraordinary speculations. Intelligences and emotions, relieved of all the imbecile preoccupations of civilized life, move in intricate and subtle dances, crossing and recrossing. . . . An immense erudition and an immense fancy go hand in hand. . . . The verbal surface of his writing is rich and fantastically diversified. The wit is incessant. . . .'

This description, one felt at the time, could well have been applied to the tales of Huxley himself. The combination of wit and erudition is an uncommon one in English fiction, and one has to go back to Peacock (by whom Huxley was much influenced) to find a comparable example. Aldous Huxley's erudition was, even in his earlier works, encyclopædic: yet he wore his learning lightly, with an off-hand, man-of-the-world air which was entirely disarming. He was often, in those days, accused of intellectual snobbery and it is true that he was capable, on occasion, of referring to such comparatively recondite figures as (say) Crébillon *fils* or Notker Balbulus with an air of casual omniscience which somewhat suggested the style of the contemporary gossip-writer ('Lady So-and-so, who *of course* . . .'). The trick, one suspects, was consciously employed, partly from a sense of mischief, partly from an amiable desire to flatter his readers. In the essay, *Vulgarity in Literature* (1930), he remarks of Paul Morand that he 'has a wonderfully airy, easy way of implying that he has looked into everything—absolutely everything, from God and the Quantum Theory to the slums of Baku (the world's most classy slums—didn't you know it?). . . .' Here, one feels, Huxley is having a sly dig not only at Morand but at himself.

If Huxley had written nothing after 1925, it is probable that he would be remembered today merely as a brilliant and somewhat eccentric minor writer comparable in stature (say) with Ronald Firbank. Judged by those early works, his subsequent development was astonishing: not only was he one of the most prolific of living English writers (his published works number between fifty and sixty volumes); he was also one of the most versatile. Novels, poetry, drama, travel-books, short stories, biography, essays—there is almost no literary form which he did not, at one time or another, attempt. His writings, moreover, cover an enormous range not only of form but of subject-matter: apart from his purely creative work, he wrote learnedly and perceptively of painting, music, science, philosophy, religion, and a dozen other topics. Yet, considering the breadth of his interests and the magnitude of his output, his work, examined as a whole, has a surprising homogeneity; nor, despite the temptations which could beset a successful author, did he ever seriously compromise with his intellectual integrity. Though a 'best-seller', he remains, paradoxically, an essentially 'unpopular' writer.

His development falls roughly into three phases. The earlier stories and novels were mainly satirical and (like the historical studies of Lytton Strachey) were largely concerned with the 'debunking' of accepted ideas and standards. Like T. S. Eliot, James Joyce, Wyndham Lewis, and others of his own or a slightly earlier generation, he was profoundly affected by the progressive breakdown of nineteenth-century ideals which had culminated in the First World War; and his predicament is reflected in these early volumes, in which the surface gaiety serves only to emphasize his underlying pessimism. Religion, conventional morality, romantic love—all are subjected to a cynical and ruthless mockery. The world of *Antic Hay* (1923) has much in common with that of T. S. Eliot's *The Waste Land* (which had appeared in the previous year): it is a world of 'broken images', where 'the dead tree gives no shelter, the cricket no relief'. Only in the realm of pure Art (it is implied) can one hope, perhaps, to discover some kind of established order to set against the prevailing anarchy. Yet the *fin de siècle* doctrine of 'art for art's sake' could never have proved finally satisfying to a man of Huxley's lively and speculative intelligence; and there is soon apparent a growing preoccupation not only with the more advanced theories of modern science, but also with psychology, ethics and philosophy.

This second phase may be said to have begun with the publication of *Proper Studies* (1927), the first of his books to be explicitly serious in intention. Thenceforward, though he continued to write novels and short stories, he assumed a more responsible role—that of the teacher, the professional philosopher—and can no longer be regarded as primarily a novelist, whose chief purpose is to entertain. During the 1930s one notes an increasing interest in politics and, more particularly, in the contemporary cult of pacifism; at the same time, he has begun to turn his attention to the Eastern mystics, and the third and final stage in his development can already be inferred from the works of this period.

Though by temperament a sceptic, Huxley always, one imagines, recognized within himself the need for some kind of religious approach to the universe; moreover, throughout his career as a writer, he showed a recurrent interest in the phenomena of mysticism. Others among his contemporaries, though sharing his initial scepticism, since became converted to one form or another of the Christian faith; Huxley, with greater intellectual honesty, refused to abandon his empirical attitude in such matters, and his approach to his later philosophical position has been cautious in the extreme. His prolonged study of the mystics has convinced him that the mystical experience itself—the individual's direct union with the Godhead—is an objective fact which can be experimentally verified; and his last works are almost all concerned, directly or indirectly, with an attempt to synthesize the existing evidence into a comprehensive system, to which he gave the name of 'the Perennial Philosophy'.

One can say, then, that Huxley progressed from a purely æsthetic, through a politico-ethical, to a predominantly religious point of view. This, of course, is a drastic simplification: in reality, his development was far more complex—for, as I shall try to show in this essay, most of the beliefs which he embraced in his maturity are latent in his earliest published works.

Aldous Leonard Huxley was born in 1894, a son of Leonard Huxley (editor of *The Cornhill Magazine*), and grandson of T. H. Huxley, the illustrious scientist; Sir Julian Huxley, the biologist, is his brother. His mother was an Arnold, and he was thus connected, both on the paternal and maternal sides, with that distinguished intellectual aristocracy which was so dominant a force in late nineteenth-century England. He was educated at Eton and at Balliol College, Oxford; after leaving the University, he taught for a while at Eton (an incongruous interlude to which he refers, disrespectfully, in *Antic Hay*), but soon decided to devote himself to writing. He married comparatively early, and spent much of his time during the 1920s in France and

Italy. He had travelled widely not only in Europe but in the East and in America. He had lived in California for many years before his death there in 1963.

His first published work was a small volume of poems; and this is perhaps a good moment to note that Huxley, though less known as a poet than as a prose-writer, was also an extremely accomplished writer of verse. These early poems are chiefly remarkable, today, for being so wholly unlike the average product of the contemporary 'Georgian' school.[1] Huxley, like Eliot before him, had plainly been much influenced by the French symbolists (his second collection of verse, *The Defeat of Youth* (1918) an admirable translation of Mallarmé's *L'Après-midi d'un Faune*); sometimes there are echoes of a rather eighteen-ninetyish romanticism:

> Shepherd, to yon tall poplars tune your flute:
> Let them pierce, keenly, subtly shrill,
> The slow blue rumour of the hill;
> Let the grass cry with an anguish of evening gold,
> And the great sky be mute.
>
> ('Song of Poplars')

Many of these early poems are, however, satirical or epigrammatic; and in the volume called *Leda* (1920), the more memorable pieces, apart from the title-poem (an ambitious and on the whole successful work in rhymed couplets), are of a similar character—for example, the 'Fifth Philosopher's Song':

> A million million spermatozoa,
>   All of them alive:
> Out of their cataclysm but one poor Noah
>   Dare hope to survive.

---

[1] So called in reference to the series of anthologies, *Georgian Poetry*, edited by the late Sir Edward Marsh.

And among that billion minus one
Might have chanced to be
Shakespeare, another Newton, a new Donne—
But the One was Me.

Shame to have ousted your betters thus,
Taking ark while the others remained outside!
Better for all of us, froward Homunculus,
If you'd quietly died!

A third volume, *The Cicadas* (1931), shows the same verbal felicity, but with a leaning towards more serious (and more formal) verse. Incidentally, two or three of the poems here reprinted appeared originally in the novel, *Those Barren Leaves* (1925), where, significantly, they were attributed to one of the leading characters, Francis Chelifer, who has more than a little in common with Aldous Huxley himself.

The first prose work appeared in the same year as *Leda*, 1920; this was *Limbo*, a collection of stories, one of which— 'Farcical History of Richard Greenow'—is in fact a short novel or *conte*, and occupies almost half the volume. This story is one of Huxley's most hilarious and successful essays in ironic comedy: the hero is a 'spiritual hermaphrodite', a Jekyll-and-Hyde personality in whom are combined an over-fastidious intellectual and a vastly successful lady-novelist. Re-reading it today, one is still astonished by its intellectual maturity and by the richness of Huxley's comic invention. Among the other six stories in the book, all extremely accomplished, may be mentioned 'Happily Ever After', in which one of Huxley's chief preoccupations becomes for the first time apparent. Guy Lambourne, the 'hero' of the story, is the prototype of many subsequent Huxley heroes—the young lover who is tortured by an irreconcilable conflict between romantic passion and physical sexuality. In later works this dichotomy will become almost obsessional: for Huxley has much of Swift's hatred for bodily functions, combined with a lively appreciation of the pleasures to be obtained therefrom.

In 1921 appeared Huxley's first novel, *Crome Yellow*, and with it he established his reputation. In many ways it remains—on a purely æsthetic level—his most successful achievement; like *Limbo*, it is an extraordinarily mature production for a young man still in his twenties; yet it has, too, all the freshness and spontaneity which one associates with an 'early' work. It is Huxley's gayest and happiest book: the graver, more responsible attitude of his later years can already be detected, as it were, in embryo, but the novel, as a whole, is a thoroughly light-hearted affair, enormously readable and, in parts, extremely amusing.

The structure of *Crome Yellow* owes much to Peacock: a number of people are gathered together at a house-party; there is plenty of incident—the characters dance, go swimming, assist at a garden fête, fall in love; but above all they talk—brilliantly, wittily and (almost) without stopping. The book is a conversation-piece, in which the characters, though sharply drawn and clearly differentiated, are employed primarily as vehicles for the prolific and highly imaginative ideas of their creator. It is a useful device which Huxley will adopt again in subsequent books, though seldom quite so successfully as he employs it here. The danger of such a method is that the action of the novel—and the characters themselves—will be swamped by the stream of conversation; in *Crome Yellow*, however, the balance is almost perfectly maintained and Mr Scogan, for example, though irrepressibly eloquent, is never allowed to become a bore.

In *Crome Yellow* Huxley presents a gallery of characters many of whom will be resuscitated, with slight variations (and under different names) in his later novels. There is the 'hero', Denis, for instance (it is difficult to refer to Huxley's very unheroic heroes without the ironic qualification of inverted commas) the typically Huxleyan young man, burdened (as he complains) by 'twenty tons of ratiocination', romantically in love yet sexually inhibited and profoundly convinced of the futility of Life and of himself. There is

Mary Bracegirdle, with her bobbed hair like 'a bell of elastic gold about her cheeks', the too-intelligent *jeune fille* whose theoretic knowledge of sex is so sadly disproportionate to her practical experience of it. In sharp contrast is Anne—uninhibited, hedonistic, sexually sophisticated—in whom one recognizes the forerunner of those *femmes fatales* (Mrs Viveash, Lucy Tantamount, etc.) who play so prominent a part in the more mature works.

In *Crome Yellow*, as I have already hinted, one can detect the germs of several ideas which will be developed in later books: a good example is Mr Scogan's prophetic description of a scientific Utopia (chapter v):

'An impersonal generation will take the place of Nature's hideous system. In vast state incubators, rows upon rows of gravid bottles will supply the world with the population it requires. The family system will disappear; society, sapped at its very base, will have to find new foundations; and Eros, beautifully and irresponsibly free, will flit like a gay butterfly from flower to flower. . . .'

This passage contains, in essence, an idea which Huxley will develop and elaborate, eleven years later, in *Brave New World*. Mr Scogan himself is, despite his loquacity, one of Huxley's best-conceived characters and the scene in which he impersonates Madame Sesostris, the Sorceress of Ecbatana, is one of the most richly comic episodes in a novel which, apart from its other merits, is certainly among the funniest in modern English fiction.

Crome Yellow derives, as I have pointed out, from Peacock; one guesses, too, that Huxley was also influenced at this period by Norman Douglas's *South Wind*, and perhaps, to a lesser extent, by the novels of Ronald Firbank.

Crome Yellow was followed, in 1922, by *Mortal Coils*, another volume of short stories. During the subsequent decade the short (or long-short) story accounted for a considerable proportion of Huxley's output, and it will be convenient to consider, at this point, his achievement in this form.

In the opinion of many critics, these shorter pieces are Huxley's most successful contribution to fiction. In his novels, he was too apt to use the form merely as a vehicle for the presentation of his own ideas; in the short stories, he shows a greater respect for his medium and, whereas his novels tended to become longer, more serious and more diffuse, his shorter tales retain much of the gaiety and the compactness of form which one finds in *Crome Yellow*. Among a large output may be mentioned 'Nuns at Luncheon' (*Mortal Coils*), 'Little Mexican' (in the volume of that name), and 'The Claxtons' (*Brief Candles*)—all admirably written in Huxley's best comic vein. The title-story in *Two or Three Graces* is also noteworthy, partly as a fascinating character study of a woman afflicted by *bovarysme* and partly for its portrait of D. H. Lawrence ('Kingham'), which may be compared instructively with the very different version of Lawrence in *Point Counter Point*.

During this period Huxley established himself as a master of the short essay, a form which has tended to decline sharply in popularity during the last thirty years or so. His first collection, *On the Margin*, appeared in 1923 and consisted mainly of pieces contributed to weekly reviews. This was followed, at intervals, by half-a-dozen other volumes, among which may be mentioned *Proper Studies* (1927), Huxley's first serious excursion into the realm of sociology and philosophy; and *Do What You Will* (1929), especially memorable for the perceptive essay on Baudelaire. Among other miscellaneous writings of this period are the two excellent travel books, *Jesting Pilate* 1926) and *Beyond the Mexique Bay* (1934), besides *The World of Light*, a satirical comedy about spiritualism. The drama is not, perhaps, a form at which one would have expected Huxley to excel; yet *The World of Light* is not only highly entertaining to read, but also extremely good theatre, as the present writer, who saw the original production at the Royalty Theatre in 1931, is able to testify. ('The Gioconda

Smile' in the volume *Mortal Coils*, has also been successfully dramatized.)

Huxley's second novel, *Antic Hay*, appeared in 1923 and created a considerable sensation, owing to its frank and detailed treatment of sexual matters; today, this would hardly arouse comment, but at that time *Antic Hay* acquired an undeserved reputation for 'obscenity' and several of the more respectable libraries refused to stock it.

It is a considerably longer and more ambitious work than *Crome Yellow* and, though it has much of the high spirits of the previous book, is more serious in intention. The scene is set mainly in London and the characters are drawn largely from the artistic and intellectual coteries of the time; many of them are thinly disguised portraits of real persons, among others the composer Philip Heseltine ('Peter Warlock'), who is easily recognizable in the character of Coleman. In structure the book is loose and episodic, though the story plays a more important part than in *Crome Yellow;* conversations are frequent and often prolonged, but here they are for the most part subordinated to the narrative. The hero, Theodore Gumbril, is an older, more worldly version of Denis, in *Crome Yellow*, and serves to illustrate, once again, the predicament of the modern intellectual torn between his youthful idealism and the inconvenient promptings of *l'homme moyen sensuel*. The book is an odd mixture of broad farce and a kind of ironic realism and one feels, at times, that the two elements are not perfectly fused: thus, the episode of Gumbril's 'patent smallclothes' and his farcical disguise as the Rabelaisian 'Complete Man', though extremely funny in themselves, strike one as curiously out of key with the more serious passages.

Yet *Antic Hay*, if it lacks the structural perfection of *Crome Yellow*, is in many respects a more important book. Of all Huxley's novels, it is the one which is most 'alive': the characters are presented more vividly and their relation to their background is more authentic than in any previous or subsequent work. Mr Mercaptan, Mrs Viveash, Lypiatt,

Shearwater—they remain in the memory as living entities, not as mere mouthpieces for Huxley's erudite and witty disquisitions. In this novel, too—in spite of its predominantly comic theme—it is noticeable that Huxley strikes a more emotional note than is usual with him: there are passages in which he betrays a feeling of romantic nostalgia (though tempered by an habitual irony) which one seldom finds elsewhere in his work. It should be noted, too, that in *Antic Hay* he is already beginning to employ a technique which, in his next few books, will become increasingly important: the technique, that is to say, of describing one form of experience in terms of another and of uniting a number of apparently diverse phenomena into a logical and self-contained unity. In the following passage Gumbril is lying in bed with his (platonic) mistress, Emily:

Very gently, he began caressing her shoulder, her long slender arm, drawing his finger-tips lightly and slowly over her smooth skin; slowly from her neck, over her shoulder, lingeringly round the elbow to her hand. Again, again: he was learning her arm. The form of it was part of the knowledge, now, of his finger-tips; his fingers knew it as they knew a piece of music, as they knew Mozart's Twelfth Sonata, for example. And the themes that crowd so quickly one after another at the beginning of the first movement played themselves aerially, glitteringly in his mind; they became a part of the enchantment.

Love in terms of Music—Music in terms of Love: it is a typically Huxleyan transposition of terms, and will be greatly elaborated in the next two novels. One may add that *Antic Hay*, like *Crome Yellow*, sometimes strikes a prophetic note—as, for instance, in the passage in chapter xxii, where Gumbril is soliloquizing after luncheon to the somnolent Mrs Viveash:

'I have a premonition,' he went on, 'that one of these days I may become a saint. An unsuccessful flickering sort of saint, like a candle beginning to go out. . . .'

Without disrespect to Huxley, I think one can infer from Gumbril's flippant words a faint adumbration of his creator's future progress towards the philosophy of 'non-attachment'.

Those Barren Leaves, the next novel, was published in 1925. Here, as in *Crome Yellow*, Huxley adopts the Peacockian device of the house-party; the background, in this case, is a villa on the Italian riviera, but the characters have a good deal in common with those of the earlier book. Thus, the would-be sophisticated Mary Bracegirdle reappears as Irene, the niece of the hostess, Mrs Aldwinkle (who, like the hostess of *Crome Yellow*, is largely a comic character); Mr Scogan is replaced by Mr Cardan, no less loquacious, cultured and concupiscent than his predecessor; the romantic Ivor of *Crome Yellow* becomes Calamy, the handsome young philanderer—and so on. In this novel, as in *Antic Hay*, Huxley introduces a number of grotesque episodes which, however, are here more closely integrated with the rest of the book. For example, the story of Mr Cardan's betrothal to a lunatic heiress and her subsequent death from food-poisoning is, if sufficiently fantastic, at least more plausible than Gumbril's pneumatic trousers; and the whole episode, in itself, is a vividly imagined essay in the farcical-macabre.

Love, again, plays a considerable part; here, however, a new element enters, again foreshadowing the direction in which Huxley is moving. In *Antic Hay*, his attitude to sexual relations is one of almost Proustian pessimism: sexuality, he seems to imply, is inherently squalid and disgusting but it is unavoidable; the philosopher, therefore, must accept it with a shrug and make the best of it. In *Those Barren Leaves*, however, he makes the young lover, Calamy, willingly renounce his affair with a fellow-guest and retire to a mountain-top where, significantly, he spends his time in philosophic meditation.

'And what' [asks the sceptical Mr Cardan], 'and what will happen at

the end of three months' chaste meditation when some lovely young
temptation comes toddling down this road . . .? What will happen to
your explorations of the inward universe then, may I ask? . . . Perhaps
you think you can explore simultaneously both the temptation and the
interior universe?'
Calamy shook his head. 'Alas, I'm afraid that's not practicable. . . .'

I mentioned Proust in another connexion and it is
noticeable that in *Those Barren Leaves* Huxley shows
signs of Proustian influence, not so much in the matter of
style (though this indeed is more elaborate than in the earlier
books) as in his delineation of character: Mrs Aldwinkle,
for instance, with her proprietary attitude to her 'view',
and to Italy in general, owes much to Mme Verdurin; and
Miss Thriplow's reminiscences, prompted by the smell of a
bay-leaf, also have a suggestively Proustian flavour.

If *Those Barren Leaves* owes something to Proust, its
successor, *Point Counter Point* (1928), is even more heavily
indebted to another French writer, André Gide, from whose
novel, *Les Faux-monnayeurs*, Huxley has frankly borrowed a number of technical devices. *Point Counter Point*
is one of Huxley's longest and most ambitious novels
and, I should say, the most perfectly constructed—though
the intricacy of its form entails a certain loss of spontaneity;
admirable though it is, it lacks some of the force and vitality
of *Crome Yellow* and *Antic Hay*.

The title provides a clue to Huxley's intention, which
is to present, by a method analogous to counterpoint in
music, a kind of multiple vision of life, in which the diverse
aspects of experience can be observed simultaneously.
(The technique has already been hinted at, as I have pointed
out, in earlier novels.) The method is best described in the
words of one of the characters, Philip Quarles. Quarles is
a novelist and keeps a journal in which he discusses, at
considerable length, the novelist's technique (this device of
the novelist-within-a-novel is borrowed from *Les Faux-
monnayeurs*):

The musicalization of fiction. Not in the symbolist way, by subordin-
ating sense to sound. . . .But on a large scale, in the construction. Meditate
on Beethoven. The changes of moods, the abrupt transitions. (Majesty
alternating with a joke, for example, in the first movement of the B flat
major quartet. . . .) . . . A theme is stated, then developed, pushed out of
shape, imperceptibly deformed, until, though still recognizably the same,
it has become different. . . . All you need is a sufficiency of characters and
parallel, contrapuntal plots. While Jones is murdering a wife, Smith is
wheeling the perambulator in the park. . . . (chapter xxii)

Point Counter Point is precisely the kind of novel which
Quarles contemplated writing. The 'contrapuntal' method
resolves itself, in practice, into a system of elaborate and
judicious 'cutting', comparable to the technique of the
cinema; many other writers have employed it subsequently
(Graham Greene, for example), but seldom on so large a
scale or so successfully as Huxley.

So far as its moral and philosophical implications are concerned, *Point Counter Point* seems to indicate a partial re-
gression to Huxley's earlier pessimism: the promise
(implied in the closing pages of *Those Barren Leaves*) of a
possible escape from the 'wearisome condition of humanity' is not fulfilled and Huxley's habitual cynicism takes on
a harsher, more ferocious quality. A new preoccupation
with violence is noticeable—the murder of Webley, the
fascist, for example (one of Huxley's few attempts at
melodrama and a not wholly successful one); death and
suffering, in one form or another, pervade the book—old
Bidlake's duodenal ulcer, the death of Quarles's little
boy, etc. With few exceptions, the characters are even
more unsympathetic than Huxley's previous creations:
Webley the fascist, Spandrell the ineffectual diabolist,
Lucy Tantamount a typically Huxleyan *femme fatale,*
though less perfectly characterized than some of her
predecessors. The most vividly-drawn character in the
book—and in many ways the most significant—is that of
Spandrell, a modern incarnation of Baudelaire (whose
personality Huxley has always found fascinating); the

Baudelairean situation is reproduced almost exactly—the
child's adoration for the widowed mother, the mother's re-
marriage to an elderly Army Officer, the boy's revulsion and
his subsequent cult for debauchery and the 'artificial
paradises' of drugs and alcohol. Yet Spandrell is more
than a mere echo of Baudelaire, for he represents (in a
fictitious and, of course, exaggerated form) an aspect of
Huxley himself to which I have already drawn attention—
the perpetually recurring conflict between sensuality and
asceticism. In Spandrell's case the conflict is presented in
its extremest and most perverse form: debauchery has
become, as it were, a moral compulsion, a prolonged and
unremitting protest against the mother's defection; Spandrell is filled with a passionate hatred not only for all moral
values but even for (among other things) the beauties of
nature. This is well illustrated in the following passage
(Spandrell has taken out an elderly and ill-favoured prosti-
tute for a day in the country):

'Lovely, lovely', was Connie's refrain. The place, the day, reminded
her, she said, of her childhood in the country. She sighed.
　'And you wish you'd been a good girl', said Spandrell sarcastically.
' "The roses round the door make me love mother more". I know, I
know. . . .'
　'Oh, the foxgloves!' cried Connie, who hadn't even been listening.
She ran towards them, grotesquely unsteady on her high heels. Spandrell
followed her.
　'Pleasingly phallic', he said, fingering one of the spikes of unopened
buds. And he went on to develop the theme, profusely.
　'Oh, be quiet, be quiet', cried Connie. 'How can you say such things?'
She was outraged, wounded. 'How can you—here?'
　'In God's country', he mocked. 'How can I?' And raising his stick he
suddenly began to lay about him right and left, slash, slash, breaking one
of the tall proud plants at every stroke. The ground was strewn with
murdered flowers.
　'Stop, stop!' She caught at his arm. Silently laughing, Spandrell
wrenched himself away from her and went on beating down the
plants. . . .
　'Down with them', he shouted, 'down with them. . . .'

Connie was in tears.

'How could you?' she said. 'How could you do it?'

... 'Serve them right', he said. 'Do you think I'm going to sit still and let myself be insulted? The insolence of the brutes! Ah, there's another!' He stepped across the glade to where one last tall foxglove stood as though hiding among the hazel saplings. One stroke was enough. The broken plant fell almost noiselessly. . . .

As in the other novels, many of the characters in *Point Counter Point* are drawn from living models—notably Mark Rampion, a full-length portrait of D. H. Lawrence. It is significant that the previous sketch of Lawrence in *Two or Three Graces* is extremely unsympathetic, not to say malicious; Rampion, on the other hand, is drawn with great sympathy, even with affection, and one feels that he is the only character in the book of whom Huxley almost wholly approves. The contrast between the two portraits is probably due to the fact that in the intervening period Huxley had become increasingly sympathetic to Lawrence's ideas. One would have supposed the two men to be poles apart—and in many respects they were; yet a strong friendship united them during the latter years of Lawrence's life, and Huxley, though never quite prepared to accept Lawrence's philosophy in its entirety, was certainly profoundly influenced by it. Himself (as he often confessed) a prisoner of the intellect, debarred by his temperament from a complete and satisfying participation in the life of the senses, Huxley doubtless saw in Lawrence's 'philosophy of the blood' a possible means of escape from his own predicament. After Lawrence's death, however, he seems finally to have rejected (if somewhat reluctantly) the 'instinctual' approach to life and in his subsequent works the Lawrentian influence becomes less and less noticeable. (It should be mentioned, however, that Huxley's introduction to Lawrence's letters[1] is probably the fairest and most balanced assessment of Lawrence and his work which has so far been written.)

[1] *The Letters of D. H. Lawrence* (1932).

Point Counter Point suffers, as I have said, from its over-elaborate construction; some of the old gaiety has gone and in the quality of the prose itself one notes a tendency to over-facility, a lack of tautness, and an increasing use of certain rather irritating mannerisms. Yet there can be little doubt that, technically speaking, *Point Counter Point* is Huxley's most considerable achievement in fiction. The interest of his subsequent novels is mainly one of content rather than of form: henceforward he will concentrate less upon problems of pure technique and will tend, more and more, to use the novel merely as a convenient medium for the expression of his ideas. I propose, therefore to deal, with the remaining novels rather more briefly.

Brave New World (1932) is a 'novel of the future', and might be described as the reverse of the Wellsian medal. 'Homo *au naturel*—' remarks Mr Mercaptan in *Antic Hay*, '*ça pue*. And as for Homo à la H. G. Wells—*ça ne pue pas assez.*' Huxley's Utopia, like that of Wells, 'doesn't stink enough', and besides being hygienically odourless, is in other respects modelled largely upon its Wellsian prototype; the difference between *Men Like Gods* and *Brave New World* lies chiefly in the point of view of the two writers. For Huxley the Wellsian Utopia, far from being a desirable state of affairs, represents the triumph of all that he most fears and dislikes: for it is a world in which humanity has been dehumanized, a world in which scientific 'progress' has been produced, so to speak, to the *n*th degree. Mr Scogan's prophecy in *Crome Yellow* has been more than fulfilled: babies are incubated in bottles and a system of strictly scientific conditioning ensures that each individual shall perform automatically his allotted function within the community. It is a totalitarian and a quasi-theocratic world: its 'gods' are Marx and Henry Ford—the latter referred to, on pious occasions, as Our Ford (or occasionally as Our Freud); in an artificially inseminated society the most obscene word is 'mother' and hygiene has become the ultimate moral value (the children are taught such variants of old-fashioned nursery rhymes as 'Streptocock-Gee to Banbury T, to see a fine bathroom and W.C.').

The theme is developed with inexorable logic and with much of Huxley's characteristically ironic humour; the end, however, is tragic—the story culminates with the suicide (in an air lighthouse in Surrey) of a 'savage' imported from one of the few remaining native reservations, where life remains on a purely primitive (and pre-Fordian) level. *Brave New World*, if stylistically inferior to his previous novels, is one of Huxley's most spirited performances; its main weakness lies, I think, in the fact that Huxley argues from an arbitrarily chosen set of premises and ignores a number of present tendencies which are quite as likely to influence the future as the ones with which he chooses to deal. Thus—as he himself admits in a new preface to the book—there is no mention of nuclear fission which had, as he says, 'been a popular topic of conversation for years before the book was written'. *Brave New World* may profitably be compared with George Orwell's *1984* which, allowing for the fact that it was written nearly twenty years later, seems a far more plausible (and even more depressing) vision of the future than Huxley's.

The same year (1932) saw the publication of *Texts and Pretexts*, a personal anthology in which the verse extracts are interspersed with notes and short essays by Huxley himself. Besides testifying to his wide knowledge of English and French literature, the book also shows Huxley in one of his happiest roles—that of literary critic and 'interpreter'.

Brave New World is Huxley's nearest approach to 'popular' fiction and probably served to introduce him to a far wider public. In his next novel, *Eyeless in Gaza* (1936), he reverts to an earlier and more characteristic manner. The first section describes the leading character looking at an album of photographs; his memory shifts to and fro over the past, as each photograph evokes a different scene or episode; and the novel, thereafter, shifts backward and forward in time, the successive chapters being arranged unchronologically—thus, from 1933 we jump to 1934, thence back to 1933, then to 1902, and so on. The method probably owes something to Christopher Isherwood's *The Memorial* (1932), which is constructed on a very similar plan; and politics plays a far larger part in this book than in the previous novels—a fact which again suggests that Huxley may have been affected by politically-minded writers of a younger generation.

The world of *Eyeless in Gaza* is still, very largely, the world of *Point Counter Point*, and the same kinds of character and situation recur; there is, however, an increasing interest not only in politics (more especially in the political aspects of pacifism) but in the doctrines of mystical philosophy. Huxley's final convictions are as yet only implicit; but the philosophical outlook implied in *Eyeless in Gaza* is already very different from that of *Point Counter Point*. It is interesting to note that the further Huxley progresses towards his ultimate goal of 'non-attachment', the more preoccupied he seems to become with the more unpleasant aspects of the human body. One would have expected the reverse to happen; yet in this novel and its successors there are a number of passages in which his 'nastiness' seemed, to many readers, almost gratuitously offensive. In his earlier books one could attribute such lapses to mere youthful high spirits and a desire to *épater le bourgeois;* recurring in his maturity, they are perplexing, and one can only assume that the progressive heightening of his spiritual vision in some way intensified, retrospectively, his old Swiftian loathing for the body and its functions. The only good life, he seems to imply, is the spiritual life; but we are 'born under one law, to another bound' and, since we are condemned to live in a world of lust and excretion, of enemas and halitosis, we should do well not to forget the fact.

Many of the political and philosophic ideas in *Eyeless in Gaza* are further elaborated, in a more systematic form, in *Ends and Means*, a long essay which appeared in the following year (1937). Here Huxley's main thesis is that, in political as in individual behaviour, the means condition the end and that therefore the much-invoked dictum' 'the end justifies the means', is demonstrably fallacious; the point is surely an important one and Huxley's elucidation of it is a valuable contribution to political thought. *Ends and Means* cannot, however, be regarded as a mere political tract for the times: it is, among other things (as Huxley says), a kind of 'cookery' book of reform and supplies an extremely comprehensive survey of the contemporary intellectual scene. The ideal goal of human effort has, as he says, been a matter of general agreement for the last thirty centuries: 'From Isaiah to Karl Marx the prophets have spoken with one voice. In the Golden Age to which they look forward there will be liberty, peace, justice, and brotherly love.' The trouble is—as Huxley sees it—that there has been no such general agreement about the means by which this ideal is to be attained: 'Here unanimity and certainty give place to utter confusion, to the clash of contradictory opinions, dogmatically held and acted upon with the violence of fanaticism.' Huxley's own solution of the problem (in so far as he attempts a solution) is in essence a religious one—the doctrine of complete 'non-attachment'. Whether one agrees or not with Huxley's conclusions is hardly a matter of great importance; the chief value of *Ends and Means* lies in the attempt to evolve some kind of synthesis from the political, ethical, and religious confusions of our age: and, as Huxley modestly remarks in his closing words, 'even the fragmentary outline of a synthesis is better than no synthesis at all'.

After Many a Summer (1939) is a comedy of longevity set in Hollywood: a scientist, attempting to prolong human life by artificial means, is confronted by an actual bicentenarian who has anticipated his own discoveries a century and a half before. Much of the novel is in Huxley's best comic manner but the philosophic divagations are inserted somewhat arbitrarily and tend to destroy the balance of the book. The same might be said of *Time Must Have a Stop* (1945), perhaps the least successful of Huxley's novels; in it he attempts the difficult feat of describing the mental processes of a man already dead; but the experiment can hardly be said to succeed.

Apart from fiction, Huxley's most substantial work to appear during the second world war was *Grey Eminence* (1941), a detailed and scholarly biography of Father Joseph, the confidential adviser of Cardinal Richelieu. This is a model of its kind and makes one wish that Huxley's excursions into historiography had been more frequent. His researches into the life and times of Father Joseph may well have drawn his attention to the events related in *The Devils of Loudun* (1952). This is a detailed psychological study of an extraordinary case of demonic possession in seventeenth-century France. It is of great interest, but here again— as so often in his later work—Huxley seems over-preoccupied with the more unpleasant physiological aspects of his subject. There is, for instance, a description of the monstrous enemas employed as aids to exorcism which recalls certain comparable passages in *Eyeless in Gaza*, and would seem to suggest that for Huxley the subject has a recurrent and somewhat morbid fascination.

During the last twenty years or so of Huxley's life, his output was hardly less prolific than formerly and the works of this period show a remarkable diversity. Essays and *belles-lettres* have on the whole predominated over fiction, but three novels were published since 1945 and it will be convenient to consider these together. *Ape and Essence* (1949) is a short book, hardly more than a *novella*. It is a post-atomic vision of the future and though the theme may seem to justify Huxley's melodramatic treatment of it, the most gloating relish with which he piles on the horrors somewhat diminishes the total impact of the story. *The Genius and the Goddess* (1955) explores a situation which Huxley had more than once dealt with before: the frequent combination of intellectual preeminence with a total inability to cope with the emotional (and, as often as not, the purely practical) demands of life. Henry Maartens is a physicist of genius, married to a beautiful wife who runs his life for him; the story is told by his younger assistant, Rivers, to the narrator, a novelist. Rivers had become the lover of Maarten's wife, Katy, at a moment when Maartens was dangerously ill; the young man is tortured by guilt at having betrayed his adored master, yet his act restores to Katy what Huxley calls the quality of 'grace', and she is thus enabled, by a kind of psychosomatic miracle, to save her husband's life. The situation, with its neat reversal of ethical cause and effect, has a typically Huxleyan irony. '*Le Cocu Miraculé.* What a subject for a French farce!' comments the narrator; but as Rivers points out, Oedipus or Lear could equally well be conceived in farcical terms.

In *Island* (1962) Huxley returns once again to the theme of Utopia. A remote island, Pala, is populated by a community whose principles of government are founded, basically, upon Tantrik Buddhism and an uninhibited but rational attitude to sex. In contrast with *Brave New World*, this later Utopian fantasy portrays a way of life many aspects of which, it may be supposed, its author would have found congenial. But Huxley, though he may have preferred the world of Pala to that of *Brave New World*, came to realize that such earthly paradises must prove finally helpless against the assault of industrialism and modern scientific techniques. This novel is, even for Huxley—who has never taken a very hopeful view of the future—a profoundly pessimistic one.

The more significant of Huxley's later writings were non-fictional. In 1946 appeared *The Perennial Philosophy*, a kind of anthology with an extensive running commentary, drawn from the writings of the mystics. Huxley's purpose was to extract from the manifold aspects of the subject a kind of highest common factor, a system of philosophy which shall include yet transcend the various methods by which men have sought to attain direct communication with God. As Huxley himself admitted, the mystical experience is, and must remain, finally incommunicable; many will dispute the validity of the mystic's claims, but whether one agrees or disagrees with Huxley's conclusions is largely, perhaps, a matter of temperament. On the other hand, there can be no doubt whatsoever about the intellectual integrity of Huxley himself. His 'conversion' (if one can use the word in this context) involved no intellectual surrender, no sudden 'act of faith'; it was the result, rather, of a prolonged and critical investigation of the available evidence conducted with the caution and objectivity of a scientist.

The Perennial Philosophy was followed by two studies dealing with the effects of mescalin and lysergic acid (LSD): *The Doors of Perception* (1954) and *Heaven and Hell* (1956). Huxley maintains that the hallucinatory states produced by these drugs are hardly to be distinguished from the 'Beatific Vision' of the mystics. This leads him to some interesting speculations as to the relationship between mind and body. Mescalin, for example, is allied to adrenochrome which, it is thought, may occur spontaneously in the human organism. 'In other words', writes Huxley, 'each one of us may be capable of manufacturing a chemical, minute doses of which are known to cause profound changes in consciousness.' The mystical state, therefore, may prove to be a mere function of the adrenal glands.

Adonis and the Alphabet (1956) is a volume of essays, all of which show that Huxley was a master of this form. The essay has become unpopular in an age of mass communications, but it was always well suited to that didactic strain in Huxley which he perhaps inherited from his grandfather. In this volume the title-piece may be singled out as particularly characteristic: it describes a visit to Syria and the Lebanon and relates the myth of Adonis to that unknown Phoenician who 'about thirty-five centuries ago . . . invented, or at least perfected, the ABC'.

Here Huxley is in his best vein and the witty, erudite writing recalls the light-hearted mood of such early travel books as *Jesting Pilate* or *Beyond the Mexique Bay*.

Brave New World Revisited (1959) is a long essay in which Huxley reconsiders his prophetic novel of 1932. Many of his predictions came true, he points out, very much sooner than he expected and the outlook gives little cause for optimism; yet it is our duty, he says, to resist the forces which menace our freedom, even though we may be (and probably are) fighting a losing battle.

It is a far cry from *Limbo* to *The Perennial Philosophy*, yet, as I have tried to show, Huxley's works, considered as a whole, reveal a remarkably consistent pattern of development. His earliest books, apparently so slight and even frivolous, contain the germs of his later and more serious productions. This internal cohesion is the more surprising in view of Huxley's enormous range of interests; one could instance plenty of modern writers whose work has the same kind of unity, but they are writers, for the most part, whose ideas operate within far narrower limits or who have some specific axe to grind. Huxley never ground an axe in his life—unless his unremitting and disinterested search for truth may be so described; yet, despite the homogeneity of his writings, he remains a strangely paradoxical figure: an intellectual who profoundly distrusted the intellect, a sensualist with a deep-seated loathing for bodily functions, a naturally religious man who remained an impenitent rationalist.

Aldous Huxley died in Hollywood, California, on 22 November 1963.

ALDOUS HUXLEY

A Select Bibliography

(Place of publication London, unless stated otherwise)

Bibliography:

ALDOUS HUXLEY: A Bibliography, by H. R. Duval; New York (1939).

ALDOUS HUXLEY: A Bibliography 1916-1959, by C. J. Eschelbach and J. L. Schober; Berkeley, Calif. (1961).

Collected Editions:

TWICE SEVEN: Fourteen collected stories (1944).

THE COLLECTED EDITION (1946-60).

COLLECTED SHORT STORIES (1957).

COLLECTED ESSAYS; New York (1958)

THE COLLECTED POETRY OF ALDOUS HUXLEY, ed. D. Watt (1969).

COLLECTED WORKS (1970-   ).

Selections:

SELECTED POEMS; Oxford (1925).

ESSAYS NEW AND OLD (1926).

ROTUNDA (1932)
—a general selection.

STORIES, ESSAYS AND POEMS (1937).

VERSES AND A COMEDY (1946).
—early poems, 'Leda', 'The Cicadas', and *The World of Light.*

ON ART AND ARTISTS, ed. M. Philipson (1960)

SELECTED ESSAYS, ed. H. Raymond (1961)

THE WORLD OF ALDOUS HUXLEY: An omnibus of his fiction and non-fiction over three decades, ed. C. J. Rolo; New York (1957).

Letters:

LETTERS OF ALDOUS HUXLEY, ed. G. Smith (1969).

Separate Works:

THE BURNING WHEEL; Oxford (1916). *Verse*

JONAH; Oxford (1917). *Verse*
—limited edition.

THE DEFEAT OF YOUTH AND OTHER POEMS; Oxford (1918).

LEDA AND OTHER POEMS (1920).

LIMBO (1920). *Short Stories*

CROME YELLOW (1921). *Novel*

MORTAL COILS (1922). *Short Stories*

ON THE MARGIN (1923). *Essays*

ANTIC HAY (1923). *Novel*

LITTLE MEXICAN (1924). *Short Stories*

THE DISCOVERY (1924). *Drama*
—an adaptation for the modern stage of Frances Sheridan's play.

ALONG THE ROAD (1925). *Travel*

THOSE BARREN LEAVES (1925). *Novel*

JESTING PILATE (1926). *Travel*

TWO OR THREE GRACES (1926). *Short Stories*

PROPER STUDIES (1927). *Essays*

POINT COUNTER POINT (1928). *Novel*

ARABIA INFELIX (1929). *Verse*

DO WHAT YOU WILL (1929). *Essays*

HOLY FACE AND OTHER ESSAYS (1929). *Essays*

VULGARITY IN LITERATURE (1930). *Criticism*

THIS WAY TO PARADISE (1930). *Drama*
—a dramatization from *Point Counter Point* by Campbell Dixon, with a Preface by Aldous Huxley.

BRIEF CANDLES (1930). *Short Stories*

MUSIC AT NIGHT; New York (1931). *Essays*

THE WORLD OF LIGHT (1931). *Drama*

THE CICADAS AND OTHER POEMS (1931).

THOMAS HENRY HUXLEY AS A MAN OF LETTERS (1932). *Criticism*
—the Huxley Memorial Lecture, 1932.

TEXTS AND PRETEXTS (1932). *Anthology*

BRAVE NEW WORLD (1932). *Novel*

BEYOND THE MEXIQUE BAY (1934). *Travel*

THE OLIVE TREE (1936). *Essays*

EYELESS IN GAZA (1936). *Novel*

WHAT ARE YOU GOING TO DO ABOUT IT? The Case for Constructive Peace (1936). *Commentary*

ENDS AND MEANS (1937). *Commentary*

AFTER MANY A SUMMER (1939). *Novel*

GREY EMINENCE (1941). *Biography*

THE ART OF SEEING (1943). *Essay*

TIME MUST HAVE A STOP (1945). *Novel*

THE PERENNIAL PHILOSOPHY (1946). *Commentary*

SCIENCE, LIBERTY AND PEACE (1947). *Commentary*

THE GIOCONDA SMILE (1948). *Drama*
—adapted from a story in *Mortal Coils*. Acting edition, 1949.

APE AND ESSENCE (1949). *Novel*

FOOD AND PEOPLE (1949)
—by Aldous Huxley and Sir John Russell.

PRISONS (1949). *Criticism*
—including the Carceri etchings by Piranesi, and a critical study by J. Adhémar.

THEMES AND VARIATIONS (1950). *Essays*

THE DEVILS OF LOUDUN (1952). *Biography*

JOYCE THE ARTIFICER: Two studies of Joyce's method (1952)
—with Stuart Gilbert; limited edition.

THE DOORS OF PERCEPTION (1954). *Essay*

THE GENIUS AND THE GODDESS (1955). *Novel*

ADONIS AND THE ALPHABET (1956). *Essays*

HEAVEN AND HELL (1956). *Essay*
—a sequel to *The Doors of Perception*

BRAVE NEW WORLD REVISITED (1959). *Essay*

ON ART AND ARTISTS (1960). *Anthology*

ISLAND (1962). *Novel*

LITERATURE AND SCIENCE (1963). *Essay*

THE CROWS OF PEARBLOSSOM (1967). *Children's Story*

Translation; and works containing Introduction, etc.:

A VIRGIN HEART, by R. de Gourmont; New York (1921). *Translation*

THE OPPORTUNITIES OF A NIGHT, by C. P. Jolyot de Crébillon, translated by E. Sutton (1925). *Introduction*

THE AUTOBIOGRAPHY AND MEMOIRS OF BENJAMIN ROBERT HAYDON (1926). *Introduction*

A VISION OF EDUCATION, by J. H. Burns (1929). *Introduction*

THE LETTERS OF D. H. LAWRENCE (1932). *Introduction*

AN ENCYCLOPÆDIA OF PACIFISM, ed. A. Huxley (1937). *Commentary*

THE SONG OF GOD: BHAGAVAD-GITA, translated by S. Prabhavanda and C. Isherwood; Paris (1947). *Introduction*

Some Biographical and Critical Studies:

ON BEING HUMAN: St Thomas and Mr Aldous Huxley, by G. Vann (1933).

ALDOUS HUXLEY, by A. J. Henderson (1935).

À LA RENCONTRE DE ALDOUS HUXLEY, by A. Gérard; Paris (1947).

ALDOUS HUXLEY: A Study, by S. Chatterjee; Calcutta (1955).

ALDOUS HUXLEY: A Literary Study, by J. Atkins (1956).

ALDOUS HUXLEY: A Cynical Salvationist, by S. Ghose (1962).

ALDOUS HUXLEY, 1894-1963: A Memorial Volume, ed. J. Huxley (1965).

THREE MODERN SATIRISTS: Waugh, Orwell and Huxley, by S. J. Greenblatt (1965).

THE HUXLEYS, by R. W. Clark (1968).

ALDOUS HUXLEY: A Study of the Major Novels, by P. Bowering (1968).

THIS TIMELESS MOMENT: A personal view of Aldous Huxley, by L. A. Huxley; New York (1968).

ALDOUS HUXLEY: Satire and Structure, by J. Meckier (1969).

ALDOUS HUXLEY AND FRENCH LITERATURE, by D. P. Scales (1969).

ALDOUS HUXLEY AND THE WAY TO REALITY, by C. M. Holmes; Indiana, (1970).

ALDOUS HUXLEY: A Critical Study, by L. Brander (1970).

DAWN AND THE DARKEST HOUR: A Study of Aldous Huxley, by G. Woodcock (1972).

WRITERS AND THEIR WORK